RACISM

IN WHITE AMERICA

DeHaven J. Alexander

Racism in White America

DeHaven J. Alexander

Copyright © 2025 by DeHaven J. Alexander

Books Academy LLC
112 SW H K Dodgen Loop,
Temple, Texas 76504
Hotline: (254) 800-1189

Ordering Information: Quantity sales. Special discounts are available on quantity purchases by corporations, associations, and others. For details, contact the publisher at the address above.

Printed in the United States of America.

ISBN-13:   Paperback
             Ebook

Library of Congress Control Number: 2

I Dedicate This to the Hood

21 Savage
Martha Stewart
Tiger Woods
Penguin Random House
Hachette
Livre
Scholastic Books
Peter Warwick
CEO President Kenneth Clearly
CFO Naoya Inoue
@thekareemreportG512 Laurence
Fisburne
Clarissa Shields The Gloat
Dick Gregory
Charlemagne The God
Jack Nicholson
Savannah Marshall
Amanda Serrano
Katie Taylor
Tyson Fury
Laila Ali
Gervonta Davis
Shakur Stevenson Charleston White
Champside
The Lakers
Jeanie Buss
Jamie Foxx
Lebron James
Stephen A Smith
Skip Bayless
Samuel L Jackson
Shannon Sharpe

ESPN
Fox News
CNN News
The Kardashians
The rock Dwayne Johnsons
Beyonce
Rihanna
Hillary Clinton
Bill Clinton
Madonna
Cristiano Ronaldo
David Beckham
Denzel Washington
Steven Spielberg
Will Smith
MLK
Adele
Key Glock
Dolph
King Von
Little Durk
Duck
First Take
Nipsey Hussle
J Cole
The Game
Walleo and Gillie A million Dollars Worth of Game
Tom Brady
Benavidez The Boxer
Match room
Go Go
And all the brothers who are holding it down keep your head up
Jeff Bezos Amazon
The Post office

UPS
Fighthype
Laker nation
Ashanti
Nelly
Eddie Hearn
Bob Arum
The View
DHL
President JFK
The Rockefeller Family
Bernard Arnault
Prajogo pangestu
Jensen Huang
Gautam Adani
Michael Dell
Mark Zuckerberg
Elon Musk
Rafaela Aponte Diamant Abigail
Johnson
Marta Schorling Andreen
Melker Schorling
L Oreal
FranÇoise Bettencourt Meyers and family
Alice Walton
Christy Walton
John Walton
Mackenzie Scott
Michelle Zatlyn
Lisa sue
Gina Rinehart
Miriam Adelson & Family
Savitri Jindal & Family Jacqueline
Mars

Susanne Klatten
The country of Switzerland
The country of Brunei Darussalam
The country of Iceland
The country of Netherlands
The country of San Marino
The country of Luxembourg
The country of Qater
The country of Mexico
Dr Dre
Agent Kim Anderson @aspirebooks.net
Publishing Department Sarah Bhati aspire books
The late great Kobe Bryant
LA lakers
Shack LA Lakers
Tupac
Biggie
The late great Roger Mayweather
My daughters
The pet dog lion
Magic Johnson
Jake Paul
Mike Tyson
Drake
Cardi B
Sexyy Red
Latto
Doja Cat
King Ryan Garcia
Jay z
GloRilla
Ice spice
Flo Milli
Megan Thee Stallion

Coi Leray
Nicki Minaj
City Girls Doechii
Asian Doll
Devin Haney
Bill Haney
Whoopi Goldberg
Coach prime
Shedeur sanders
Shilo sanders
Travis Hunter
Deontay Wilder
Dr Umar Johnson
Lil Kim
Missy Elliott
Queen Latifah
Mc Lyte
50 cent
Eminem
The parliamentary republic of Singapore
The country of Norway
The country of Denmark
The country of United States
The country of Saudi Arabia
The country of United Arab Emirates
Big Moe
Lamont
Big head
Golden Boy
Top Rank
Jeff Mayweather
The Honorable Minster Louis Farrakhan
Snoop Dog

Floyds Grandson Kentrell H
money Boxing
Kock Out boxing 86 TV
Prince
Michael Jackson
Michael Jordan
President Barack Obama
Michelle Obama
The Nation Of Islam
ALLAH
Oprah
Tyler Perry
King Abdullah
Queen Elizabeth II
President Vladimir Putin
Emperor Akihito
Prime Minister Xavier Bettel
President Micheal D Higgins
President Tharman Shanmugaratnan
Prime Minister Mette Federiksen
President Alexander Van Der Bellen
President Viola Amherd
President Paolo Rondelli
President Mohammed bin Zayed Al Nahyan
President Tamim bin Hamad Al Thani
President XI Jinping
President yoon Suk Yeol
President Frank Walter Steinmeier
President Kim Jong Un
Kim Yo Jong
President Sergio Mattarella
President Luiz Inacio Lula da Silva
My wife Claudia G Alexander The
boxing voice

Ring walk Dany and Nestgto
Lamont at large
Good fella TV
PBC
Lakers Nation
Monnie Brown TV
Indisputable with
DR. Rashad Richey
Blue Blood Sports TV
Wille D Live
Geddy Radio Show Ceddy
Nash
Colorado Football
BOXINGEGO
TRUESULTS
Jaye De Black
Get hip TV
Everything Boxing
CE CE REACTS
THE KAREEM REPORT
Taylor swift
J Prince
Canelo Alvarez
Fannon International Boxing Channel
The queens of boxing
President Biden
President Donald Trump
Turki Alalshikh
Gene Deal
Whack 100
Chris Brown
My grandson Ezekiel
Cam and Mase
78 the general

Floyd Mayweather Sr. and Jr.
My sons.
Big Moe
Willie D,
let's go.

PS: I left out another guy who knows what he's talking about the General.
And Cam and Mase, and Gene Deal, and Everything Boxing

Racism In White America

I am not going to explain the history of Black men, I will get straight to the point. I think by now everyone knows who has the upper hand in life, but not to make excuses. The Black man needs to take care of his business. The family has to come first: wife and kids. The problem is men need to take care of their business in the Home.In his business, if he can't reach his goals, he blames it on the white man. I think if you put yourself in a bad position, you will get bad results. The Black man has a criminal record and a drug problem; he can't find a job. That isn't the white man's fault; it is your fault. The white man doesn't want to hire you over another white man, so you are making his job easy.wag up am not saying all Europeans are like that, just most. The Black man has to take care of his priorities, and then he will be able to take care of his family. People of all backgrounds value money, and sometimes they like to interact with women who are unattractive and overweight.

because these women are easy to have sex with. I am not talking about all Black men, just most. And this can go for all men. The problem we have is that once you get these women pregnant, you make a baby that you don't want, and now you have the baby daddy. The kid is the one that gets hurt in the end. I think women can also be a problem.

and now you have the baby daddy. The kid is the one that gets hurt in the end. I think women can also be the problem. Women of all races need to raise their standards when dating men. Women who are at the bottom of the socioeconomic class often have low standards, not all but most. They date guys who are on their level. I think they should get it together, and maybe they can meet better men. Worked with a white guy,and he told me The only way his daughter could date a Black man Is if he was a Republican because he knew He would have a good job and no baby mamas. The Black community and all races have a problem with mistreating women, pimping women. How could you pimp a woman? This is all races of men. The men who treat women like that are the ones who are scorned and broken down. I think if you are a woman and you want to sell your body, work for yourself, not for other women or men. This is the most disrespectful thing I have ever seen in my life. I think laws need to be more disciplined for this crime. Women need to band together and form their own protection for themselves and cut out the pimp. I can't blame this on racism because you have all races doing this. Women need to be strong and support each other. This is backward. Everyone is obsessed with money; the more money, the better your life, so we think. Money cannot buy you love or happiness. The Black community has been sold out for years.

One was a sex worker-those women would have been locked up under the jail because they were Black and Asian. And they killed a white man-sec the point? And you know I am correct. Sam Cooke wasn't the only Black man murdered;We can look at Prince and Ml,And the list goes an and on.The European has one God,and that is money,Then his family,then God-that is the way he thinks.The white man makes a lot of money off drugs and guns.The reason we have a lot of deaths and violence a lot of money can be made off guns and drugs.I think the European lets a certain amount of drugs and money stay in the system,then clamps it down when you have to make an arrest.The Black man wants to be rich and famous like mast men,But the Blacken will get the most time.The system is set up to play out that way. I think in some of these states down south, they still will give the Black man a hard time.

The laws are different in the case of a Black man and a white man. I do not have to name the states, but you know what I am talking about-just do your research. Black men can be different; you have some Black men who do not want to accept their race. I've seen Black men date white or Asian women only, and I've seen white men who date Black women. I don't see anything wrong with that as long as you don't forget where you are coming from.

The saddest situation I have seen are Black people, men and women,He retrying to fit into another race. A Black man who has white friends and tries to act white.The white female who acts Black and talks Black and has Black boyfriends.A guy told Leif he's dating a white girl,he wants her to act like Becky or Susan-He didn't want her to act like Ha Na Na,or a hood rat.

The way you change,the only way you Will contain racism is to work on the kids. The parents are a waste of time;they are growing up In generation of racism. The way you can change the problem is to work on the young kids before they reach their teens. Kids are easy to influence when they are young. The white race is not dying out; that is why they are breeding with the Mexicans, to keep the race growing. One day, racism could shrink if we can stop these kids from being brainwashed. The Black man's problem starts with the family structure in the household.The Black man was raised by his mother and big mama most of the time. Food is a big problem most of the time. The man will do whatever he has to do to feed his family. I understand you have to do what you have to do. The Black man has to think from day one that you are Black, so you have one strike. Females have two strikes -you are Black, and you are a female. The reason I state that is you have to think outside the box. The Black man needs to continue his education to the highest level, stay out of trouble, or go into the military. I think everyone should follow these steps, but Black people know they are starting from behind, so don't put yourself in a hole. Females have a say in what is going on in this world. you want that fast buck, so you date men With an josh but they have money because they are criminals. Sometimes they have an education or a good job.

The female loves the houses and cars but doesn't get a chance to Know the Guy. Then nine months later, you find out he's married or a criminal - it is too late. That is the problem with our women; their mothers didn't school them right, most of the time.

I think these young girls are messed up in the hood; They will do anything to get that bag, as they say on the street. The girls of today are wasted. Like a female who keeps herself up, by today's standards, you don't know what is real on the women these days. I blame this on the parents - A lot of Black and all races are not paying attention to how the world is changing. Digital will change the world; a lot of people, all races,Dante have bank accounts. The government will control the money flow, which is a good idea. Taxes will be paid;the digital will eliminate the drug boys; there will be no such thing as cash. I am not saying this will hurt the Black race -it will hurt all races. I know we all know people who live in one state and have tags in another state;This digital mane will stop that and save money for each state. The race who has the most uneducated people will Hurt the most. The Black man has a big problem with the way he is treated in sports. The guy who beat the case in Florida on self-defense when he was attacked at his home. I think he will never get back in the league; it will bring too much negative press. The owners will blackball him out of the league. I think that would happen to any player, but because he is Black, it won't help his case.

I think if the league had its way, it would want all the players to be white, but there are too many great Black players to make that happen. I have seen a lot of Black QB -Cam and Kan-out of the league. They'd rather have a sorry-ass white

QB making millions on the bench -these guys suck. cam and K Er, are better than these guys.They don't want to win; they just want to make money, some owners.Apostleship to Attending the games and view the games on TV;that might bring awareness. Blacks,l am talking about ownership,will never happen because the white owners pass away And they leave the teams to their kids, and they pass it on. The phase is selling the team to a white owner;this wile block the Black man out.The NBA is a good league for ownership; they know the Black man helps that league out. I hope one day the NFL brings awareness to the problem because it is a big problem. President Obama ran for President; a lot of Black people voted for Obama who had never voted before.There were Black people who voted for Obama because he was Black, and they thought he

Was going to provide free chicken dinners and fish fry every month. The white establishment put Obama in office because they knew he was going to get the Black vote. I am not saying Obama wasn't a good president; he was able to do so much. I thought he was going to help get the bad cops off the streets. I know they say cops only kill Black people. That is bullshit; they kill more white people than Black people; that is the media. There are more white people on Earth.The media only covers the Black shootings because They will get more coverage.The Memphis police got a lot of coverage because they are Black.Black cops killing Black guys, so that tells you it is not a Black problem, just a police problem. I think they should use the lie detector to help process when it comes to hiring police police. The process isn't working; they need to find another way. Too many bad cops are slipping through the cracks. The bad guys are hiring bad cops to be on the payroll. Crime will never stop.

Is too much money to be made off guns and drugs.I think Trump will help the country because he speaks his mind. The country was better off when he was in office because He didn't let other countries bully the USA.The day Trump gets back in office, the food and gas prices will come back down because Trump will stop giving all that money to other countries and help the Americans out. I have no problem with helping other countries out. I think we need to help our country out first. The USA needs to do a better process when it comes to letting people enter. I would like to see everyone go to a country of your choice and see how hard it will be to get aid and housing and food if they allow you to enter the country. The process needs to be fixed. The Black community needs to support their people's brands. Black people will wear a lot of high-priced brand fashions, but they won't support Black brands. Women will do anything to wear a high-priced bag instead of taking that money and buying land or investing the money to make more money. Women will go to the Asian nail shops instead of supporting their own people's businesses;those Asians don't care a damn about you. I remember years ago,an Asian lady killed a young Black girl in LA;the Asian lady got off free. I think Black people need to stick together and support their people and be supportive of each other, like the other races. I was watching a comedy show, and Ernie Mac said there were three guys: a Black guy, a Black guy, a white guy. The Black guy went to the gate to try to get into Heaven. The Mexican guy told the Black guy, "You know God won't let you in because you are bad." The Black guy went to the gate to speak to God, and God said, Open the gate." The Mexican guy asked God, 'Why did you let him in?'""God told the Mexican, "He asked me a question I didn't know the answer to."

The Mexican guy said, "What was that?" " God told the Mexican, 'Tell me, when will all black people get along with each other?" God said,"1 didn't know the answer.' I told them to let him in."The only way we can try to fix the problem is to try to teach the young kids about racism. Kids are not born hating different races; it is a sad situation. I remember when in the military, I was in Basic training. I met a white guy named Becker; we became good friends. He told me he never had A Black friend. He told me his father didn't like Black people,but his mother wasn't like his father.He was from Missouri.I wondered what ever happened to him;he probably married a Black lady.He might have Black kids.Kids have a hard time growing up without dads,all kids,Black AR white. I know a situation where the little girl, a Black girl, has no dad. The mother does everything in her power for the little girl; the girl is 14 and she has a bad attitude towards everybody.The little girl will get in your car and doesn't speak.She told me she doesn't like to speak to people. But this is the kicker: she can come over to your house, she can ride in your car, and car and accept things from you, but she doesn't like to speak to you. 1 also noticed she goes over to her boyfriend's house and speaks to his family, but when she goes out of town to visit her family, she doesn't speak. The boyfriend is 14;she is 14.The mother lets the little boyfriend come over and go into the room, But they have to keep the door open.The problem we have is mothers going outgo their way to Please their daughters because there isn't a father in the house. I think this is a bad signal to your daughter. A lot of little girls, Black and white, come out messed up because they are confused.

I think you have to be strong with these girls and set the rules because if you don't,another mouth To feed will be on its way. I watch YouTube,and I see kids,Black and white,cursing at the parents And the siblings.I never see Asian kids do this behavior;mostly it's the Black and white kids because The parents think this is funny.The community is messed up;it wile never change until the parents change. Then you can work on the kids.I know you can't control a man's actions or how raiser es his kids. know the government cannot get involved in that.All they can do is put a man on child support. Men seem to get around that,in some cases,women also.The key to the situations if women would Take their time and stop chasing money and just date a better man and use birth controls Until you know he is the right guy,maybe that problem could be in a better place. Girls are getting pregnant at a very young age;if you have two 15-yearolds having baby, 9 out of 10 times the baby will grow up in a bad situation if you don't have a good support system. The parents are the backbone of this situation,mostly the mother,because most of the time there Is no man in the home when you are dealing with a Black family.The man can make or break a Family;it depends an what type of man the female has in her life.If she was raised without a Daddy,sometimes she doesn't have guidance on how a woman should be treated.A lady can raise kids,but a man would help the situation become easier.I watch a lot of different problems that are going on in this world.I don't understand why Black people put themselves in bad situations with the police.The best thing to do is sit, Listen,and follow instructions;don't go back and fart because you have to remember, A lot of police are from small towns where they didn't grow up around Black people. think they believe we are all bad and are criminals.The few times I was pulled over, The cop was scared and shaking;that is why I stayed calm.I know this guy is scared to death. The mall cops are scary;he is the guy that couldn't become a policeman and he has a raja, Spray,and handcuffs,and all the gear,and if he has a gun,watch out.I think sometimes they are worse than a cop;they are waiting to use their polices on You I mentioned before they need to find a better way to select policemen.I think guy we has been in Trouble and came up in the hood would make a better policeman.The reason I believe that is He saw both sides of the law,and he didn't want to go back to some guys,not all guys.The policemen with the clean records seem to be the bad cops.I think you can take the small-town Guy who was a fat kid growing up;the guy got on the force and realized he has so much power And he hangs around bad cops and then he gets caught up in the game.I think the movie Training Day is a good example.I can look back at the MLK days with the marches and being sprayed with Water hoses.The Black man and women went through so much in those days;such a bad situation.The white man paid the Indians reparations because they took their land .I hear they are talking about doing that for Black people.I think if that happens,you are going to have so many races trying to be Black,and if they give that money to Black people,most people will give The money back by spending it an dumb stuff.I think everyone knows if you give"niggers"a lot of money At one time,the government thinking they have problems,everyone will be Neo Brown Houses,cars,everybody will have a Cadillac;you know how "niggers"are.

I would take my mane and Buy land and homes,fix them up to sell,and try to help the homeless.I would take my money and turn it into generational wealth,but that is just me.think that will never happen;the white man won't let Black people come up like that,but it is a good thought. I think Black people need to focus on the problems that are going on around their community. Black people need to boycott these restaurants that are racist to Black people.Denny's and Apple bee's just for the start.I can't see how a Black man is sent home because he came to work early.The white lady is a racist and the district manager too;both of them are racists.This took place at the Apple bee's.Denny's have their problems also.Black people need to only eat at Black restaurants And support each other's businesses.The only way we can stop those problems into hurt their pockets.They will have Black Friday every week to give back to the African American community.The problem won't be addressed;they will play around it because they know the African community Loves to eat.The Black community has to band together and just spend your money an Black businesses is the only way to solve the problem.The community can solve the problem if they stop spending your mane on these white businesses;that will be the only way.The youth of today is stupid and dumb;all they care about is drinking and smoking, And hoking up,pepping bottles,club chasing,and dressing in name brand clothes.

I think this problem starts with the parents.The parents are having kids at a young age, A young age,and they act just like they are kids.I remember back in the day when l used to Go out l knew females who had kids,and today they are going to the clubs withthairDaughters.I heard of females sleeping with her daughter's boyfriend's friends.Iam not saying That is in the Black community;that is in every community.The churches are another problem. The pastor wants you to pay all these tithes to God.But the money goes to the pastor so he can buy a fancy house and cars and live in big houses.I am not saying this is every pastor, But damn near every pastor.The only way we can control this problem is we need to spend time with our kids and also start programs for kids like that movie "Billy Jack." The people in the community had programs for all kids.I think if you get to thesis at a young age You might can stop same of these kids before they turn out like their parents,Black and white. I remember when I was in the military,there was a guy from Missouri.He told heme never had a Black friend;his father didn't like Black people,but he said his mother wasn't thataway. l am touching up on that story l explained earlier in the book,I think his name was Becker. He is probably sitting back,playing with his grand kids,eating some watermelon.He reminded me of a guy I used to work with in the post office named Joe Parker,a nice country boy, A good guy, Joe Parker married an Indian lady named

Sonya, a nice lady; they made a nice couple I always thought they had the blueprint on how to make a marriage work.

God made every person the same way;we are just different colors.Whatever god you believe in,There is only one gad.I hope the community bands together and supports their community.stop supporting other communities that don't support your community.Denny's-how many times have the Black community been disrespected by these People: fl you stand up and ban Denny's and Apple bee's,I bet they would take a closer look At the problem.I think if we stand up and stop eating at Denny's and Applebee'sbecause They don't like Black people,but they will take our money. I remember I saw the news about a Black man sent home early by a white femaleness Because he came to work early;she should be fired.I can write all day about these white businesses that treat Black people like shit.The ably way we can get their attention is to spat spending our money And support our own businesses.The Black community spends money an everything from Cars to clothes to food;if we can boycott these businesses and spend money honour own community, t will make them change their minds cal quick.I want to tall about the NFL;all these Black players and no Black owners.I guess they know people love football and they don't care. Just think if Black people and players boycotted the games,they would award a Black person Team.I am tired of watching these white QB who suck and they ride the bench and Get paid forty million,and you have Cam and Kan.siting at home who are being blackballed Far speaking their mind.Hockey can have a pass;Blacks don't play hockey,maybes few.The NFL is a white society that keeps the teams in the family.

No Black man and woman will ever own a team. Black people don't care,and they know we spend a lot of money on the sport,from watching it to betting and attending the games Blacks are not educated on this kind of problem;some of us are not business-minded.We like to spend mane and support other groups.They put a song out that says,"If l only had a brain."Black people need to band together and Put our mane together and open our own banks and loan companies.I would like to see All millionaires and billionaires band together and start our own business and helpeveryaneWho is trying to buy homes and cars and attend illegal.I would like to see Blacks open schools and colleges.The Black man can be very powerful;we can start our own Flack NFL and have Black everything. I bet if we had a business mind,they would take note.I heard a billionaire was giving to give Kobe a line of credit worth a billion dollars to start his own league.don't have to explain what happened.I don't know if this is the truth,but that is what I heard.I hope that wasn't the truth,but since we are an the subject.I heard they killed Whitney Houston because she was asking about her masters.She was going broke,so she started asking about her money.They found her with Bruises all over her body in the bathtub.I heard they found Jimmy Hendrix dead in the bathtub.haven't heard a lot of strange deaths about whites,but I bet there are a few out there.James Brown,Prince,MU all died going through problems with retard label problems.The devil is alive;I know this sounds strange,just do your research.can tall about the problems we are having with racism.

The problem is Black people need to support each other and help each other out.You will never stop the hate,but if you stop buying their goods and supporting their Business,that will send a message,and they might change their ways because the Black Race spends the most money an bullshit.The young Black people need counseling Because they are the solution in trying to salve this problem.First of all,buying these Fancy watches and cars,let's just say ten people got together with millions dollars.The people took that mane and bought land,and every time they wanted to bullishness,They bought land.

Ten years later,people come to them wanting to buy that land.Or keep the land and build homes or rent the land.Now you have money coming In all the time,so if you want to buy that bullshit,you have the money to replace the bullfighting you used to purchase the bullshit.I wish I could put a summit together all over the world,with all of the billionaire sand millionaires,schools,banks,and loan companies;we could build our own enterprise.That will never happen;they will shut that down kraal quick I was listening to a guy online who goes by the name of Insatiably.He made sen seat what He was talking about.He was talking about an 80-year-old judge who was married 50 bears guy one day found out that his kids weren't his kids;he had two sons,they were 40 and 42 .I don't know if his wife was still living.Anyway,he was saying the sons are deadbeats,and He is still supporting them.The judge said he is filing a lawsuit to get his child support guy on the chat was saying we need to be more careful about who we predating because, This is what happens when you step out while being married.A woman will pay the precarious she will be stuck with the baby.What is wrong with condoms?We live in a stupid World with dumb people,men and women;this happens every day,all races.I use the N-word a lot,but there is a difference between a nigger and a Black man.

The white man gave us that name back in slavery.A nigger can be any race because nigger is a law down piece of shit like a deadbeat baby daddy.The list can go on and on.I have met people who let that bother them;learn your history,that ward shouldn't bother you.The white kids call each other that all of the time;they are trying to be cool.Understand if Some white guy called me that to my face,then I understand.I was aniline one day,and a guy was talking about a lady who was living with him for years And he raised her daughter.The daughter was getting married;the guy was paying for everything 250 people were coming to the wedding at his house.He wanted 20 of his friend sand family To come,but the girl's mother said 20 people was too many.The girl invited her deadbeat dad To walk her down the aisle,not the guy who raised her;he hasn't done anything far the girl.I was stating our young girls are not being raised right because the women of today,some-Not all-are fucked up in the head;something went wrong with them,then the daughters after them.The guy did the right thing;he kicked the daughter and the mother out of his house-thank God he didn't marry the lady.I was thinking she was probably still fucking The baby daddy.Females and men of today, Why are these young rappers killing each other left and right?I think it is designed for flack people To kill one another left to right I think guns should be banned altogether,but they make so much money off guns,you will never see that happen.The problem is carrying guns and using them when you get mad.The lady who fallowed the Black Guy and shot him and murdered him.She was trying to be a policewoman.They told her to stop Fallowing him.Just leave;they will take care cf the rest.she was big and thought she was a badass.The problem is when you put guns in people's hands,it does something to them;it gives them power.The people who carry guns,most of them can't fight,so they carry guns.

They feel tough.I see police Ladies,Black and white,yell and curse at people for no reason.They have that gun,and their them tough.I think that is a dangerous job,and some people shouldn't bebops.I think sometimes they are scared,men and women,that is why they pull the trigger.White women haven't been through what a Black woman has;that is why they scaremonger they get around Black people.You can take some people who grew up in the had,And they would make better caps,Black or white.People take a white woman;she went to College,lived in a nice community;she is the worst cop working in the hood,no experience Around Black people.I think you have some good cops,but you have a lot of bad cops.The bad cops are racists,and they shouldn't be policemen or women.I think if spokespeople keep guns in the home,a lot of people would still be alive.

The only people who should be allowed to carry firearms are law enforcement because they are trained IE use firearms.The world would be a better place to live if the gun laws were better and they did better job selecting The officers of the law.They shoot as many white guys as Black guys.The media just picks the Black shootings because that Brings more attention to the news media.They need to come up with a device that can tell if a policeman or woman is lying.I think the lie detector would be perfect because if you are giving any signal that you are lying.That will let them know that person might not be a good candidate for the job.I think a person can be good,but when they get that power,it makes them cocky.The person may never have been around Black culture,and that creates a problem When they are in public.I've been pulled over by cops with bad attitudes.I remember one time I was asked what I did For a living because I had a nice car.I am pretty sure they thought I was a drug dealer.The look on his face when he saw l was a Tax-paying citizen.I think you have Black and white bad cops.The problem needs to be fixed soon because one day The world will target police,and they will have a hard time hiring good cops.Iam going to break the problem down case by case.I am not trying to tell Black people support white businesses,just the bad businesses.I know Black people know what is going on;they just don't care until it happens to them or a family Member.I think Black people have the power and wealth to support Black businesses.Housing is a big problem;the government put a lot of mane into people jumping the border.Take that money and help our people get on their feet;then when they pay their taxes,That money will be put back into the system;then you can help people case by case.

One year later,the boyfriend's in jail,The girl has another man,and she's pregnant by him.He isn't paying any attention to her other two kids.One day,she's complaining to me,Then tries to slip her number to me.I took the number,went back to my truck,And threw tin the trash. I said to myself,"I know she's got allure,But iI'm not trying to get caught in the game."Misremember time,the Mather was with Her daughter's baby daddy's friend. This is the type of drama that unfolds in this community.I think I've pinpointed nae reason Why some women struggle to find a man here.I don't think a high-level man wants a woman an welfare With multiple children from different fathers, And troubled kids,while she's on welfare. The women who look nice might catch a man's eye,But all he wants is to have his way with her. The men who marry these women re bums with no life,just laying up in these women's homes Until they can find the next come up The married woman hangs out with her girlfriends, Who sometimes don't have the best interest in her marriage.I've heard of situations when they go on trips, ND the girlfriends meet guys who want to take them an a boat,Or to their houses. The married woman has to make a decision: Should she let her friends go and stay back?But most will go because they want to fit in.

They go an,but they tell those guys they are married.Now,you're in another country.Telling a man you're married.This man will do what he can to win you over,Even if you resemble someone as famed as the Guardianship.He'll go all out,thinking to himself,"Forget your husband."And perhaps,the woman might think the same,glacially if the man has money. The women who claim they don't need a man,Paths they need to work on themselves. if you're overweight,that might be why You wear a size 12 but insist on buying a size 9.Then some of you with those wild hairstyles, And outrageous makeup-no high-class man wants that,In my best impression of Kevin Samuelson. cl Godailla wallabys sais,No man gants a soman ho looks lie a clown. I think Big Mama raised her daughter well, But then her daughter didn't do the same. Now,we're stuck in a cycle with these girls Having babies with irresponsible boys,And it goes on and on. I think the only way this will stop is if the government steps in to solve these problems Make all money digital,so taxes and child support Are automatically deducted-no way to dodge it. The government should mandate birth control for all girls until they're 21, And require registration for marriage along with two years AF counseling. The rates of divorce and unplanned parenthood would drop, And if there are children, support payments would be automatic.Programs like food stamps and housing assistance might decrease,Freeing up more money to help the homeless. I know I might be getting off topic, But the root of these problems starts with parenting. This is why we have all these issues.

The ladies who don't want a man are not into men, But mast women do want a man-they just can't find the right one.First things first:get yourself together. There's a guy named charlatan White who speaks his mind on many topics.l appreciate his candor-just wish he'd steer clear of discussing certain individuals.Though not everyone likes him,they should consider his points; He's often telling the truth. White women face similar challenges as Black women.Mexican and Asian families often stay together;They don't have many fathers to their children but some, Raising large families together and working hard-A practice that should be passed down to Black families.These women need to consolidate their finances,They're spending too much on retail. They should be buying land and investing. One day,I hope we can have a summit about all these issues.If you're spending that kind of money on cars and retail,Invest itin your community to elevate everyone,That will lift both youand your children The biggest problem we face is lack of support within our cwm race;We need to stand together and assist those who strive to succeed,But as it often goes,everyone wants to be the first and only. I know some might question why l use the N-word.l use it because it grabs attention. A Black man is just a man,like a white man;A nigger is nothing but trouble. White kids use that word trying to be cool,Until they say at the wrong time. A woman Who likes Black men shows me She wasn't raised in a prejudiced home,Or she grew up and made her own decisions.

I've seen White girls who avoid Black men,Knowing they couldn't bring nae home. I remember overhearing a White girl call me handsome,But too dark-l had to laugh, As I've heard the same from Black women.Like my man Eid said,"They got the vapors."During slavery,White men took Black women,And White women took Black men. It's still happening today,and l love seeing A Whitman with a Black brother. 1 don't feel the same about a Black woman with a White man;I think she's putting down Black men because she thinks the White man Superior. The white woman,when she is with her brother,is putting herself in the spotlight.Family,friends,and coworkers,why are you with that nigger that is probablygoing through Their mind,but the white woman doesn't care about it because she cares about that black man. Even though she knows she will not hear the end of it.Black women will haveprgblems Also,think would accept her being with the white guy because they look at her asbeing With the master,they are looking at that white woman as why you with hatemonger. The black woman thinks she is on top of the world because she is the master AF allot her. Problems are solved that might be in some cases,but they don't like your black ass either. You better wake up and smell the caffeine.I think kids don't go through the same adults because they don't know the shit.They are kids. The white race is dying out;they don't want to see white women with a black manor any man. Out of their race,but I think they would accept the Mexicans because they kiss the white man's ass.

I was told in the year 2050,the white race will be the smallest,and the black race will Have the most people an earth.I heard they are buying up all the land to plant bad food. That will stop the black race from growing by making it hard for black women Mohave kids. if this is true,it might backfire.Oak how big these kids are growing;these girls, 13,are They look like they are 21,but you can look in their face and see they look like babies.I don't Understand why a grown man wants to be with a 13-year-old.The Boys are big form Eating that food that they are growing.!I hear a lot of women of all races that predating these Young guys are doing the same thing that the men are doing. These school teachers are sleeping with these little boys because I guess rebirthing as a grown man from eating that food. Told you it is the food they grow,meant to kill the black man's sperm. I think the plan will backfire,indeed,if true,because all races share this feed,and hence the problem will all races bleed.That's why you see these Amazon kids arise. I think these pastors in the church run wild,not all,utmost;their ways are far from mild. I refuse to pay tithes for pastors to drive fancycars,live in mansions vast, and attempt to seduce your wife and daughters.This isn't made-up;it's seen every day. I want name names,but rumors fly of sex parties,and all that church-housed nonsense plays. No need to give them ten percent of my hard-hearted ways. l admire when shat goes out,buys bikes,toys,and food for those in need that's the kind of help that truly feeds.

I see big churches gathering the most mane,both black and white,it's not even funny.await the usual nonsense from the pastor,brainwashing by church disaster. Some churches want only the wealthy far members.I don't know much about white congregations,but malware of the black perspiration,pretty sure they're all cut from the same cloth.I watched on YouTube, at a funeral,no less,a procrastinating with a ring,oh the mess-must've been sleeping with the widow, I guess. knew a lady,newly widowed,rich and free,married her pastor-see the trend? These snake-like pastors,their reach extends,both black and white,their morals bend. think the country would heal,could we blend,support each other,regardless of skin, in black and white,together begin.I've been to a soul food place,where whites dine no tout of grace but taste. Yet some order out,avoiding the place,liking the food,not the race- the hypocrisy in their embrace. Consider how many climb using beds as ladders,black women with white bosses,sad but true,low-life games,with marriage vows askew. Sex sells;many use their bodies,aiming higher,better than giving it free,then left with a baby,dire. l believe men who neglect their kids lack proper upbringing,missing the basics. Why do men dating mothers shun the kidskin? Is It distrust in his lady, a love that fades? Better to know now than later,caught in the act,a problem old as time, this painful fact. Had he given space, she might've shown her face, I've never faced it, but it happens, a common space.

I wane talk about the problems with the music and Hollywood business.I can't understand why you have all of these rappers and entertainers making allot this money and they're not trying to band together to build their own platform.I was told a lot of these entertainers have in theircontract that they can't help their people.The baser Tank bought the block in Baltimore Where he live sand they burned some of the buildings down. The reason why nobody is trying to help the black community is they can't because they aren't allowed to help their people out.Look what happened to Bill Cosby.He was trying to buy NBC.I haven't heard from him since he got out of that mess.guess he knew to just chi and enjoy what he has left for the remainder cf his life. I remember I got sick and I went to the hospital and they were trying to give me these shays. I told them the minister said don't take those shots and they released me fram thehospital I think the reason why a lot of black entertainers don't make a platform is because they are scared. The devil is alive and he will bring you down.I know a lot of people are scared Rostand their ground. Because they have a lot to lose,I guess money is everything and to some people,they care about money mare than their family. The world is run by devils and all you can do is play their game and wait until you get a chance to get that bone tossed your way. guess if you speak your mind,you will face a lot of bad problems coming your way.Well,l always say what is on my mind because sometimes the truth hurts.guess if everyone stopped,looked at what is going on,and tried to treat people fair,it won't change the world,but it might help the problem.

The black community will never make it to the top because we are trying to outdo each other,they is why we will never make it-sad. The community needs to wake up and look at what is going on. They are slowly trying to take back what we have and change the laws to take back what we have,and change the laws to favor back to the white man.Schools will change the laws to favor back to the white man,school swill change,voting will change. The next thing we know,we will be back on the boat in chains.The community only cares about material goods and parties-just look around and see how blacks try to live and spend their mane on bullshit. The women don't know how to pick a good man;all they want is the ballets.The black man just wants to date super and nice-looking girts. At the end of the day,everyone loses. The mothers of the daughters are sleeping with their daughters'boyfriendsbecause he had money. I remember back in the day,we knew this lady;she was around35 and her daughter was 16.The lady was dating this drug dealer around 22.The drug boy paid the lady's rent and car note. The lady did not realize the boyfriend was sleeping with her daughter.I never knew how that turned out but I guess it went for the worst. am going to get deep into the problems we have in the black community,the white community. When it comes to mother and daughter relationships,are much better,I think,because the white mother wants her daughter to meet a nice man and get married and support her daughter and kids. The white women will go out of her way to make sure her daughter or son will have a home, for their family, even if she has to help purchase the home. Sometimes she can get to involve and it might make the spouse fill to uncountable I know a situation where the lady is in her forties with two kids who lives with her mother. The lady warks,her mother warks also,but her mother seems not able to keep a job. The mother moved in farm out of town when her daughter's failed relationship her Baby daddy did not work.The mother loves to gamble and the daughter goes with he to play a little and watch but mostly watch.

The daughter met a guy who she is dating for three years and the plan is for the both of them Ia buy a home. The daughter stays in the house that she rented out and her mother pays half therent. The mother has been married twice and she is still married to the secand husband.The mother is like P Diddy she ahways want to be on the records and all in thevideos That type.The daughter doesn't want to live with the mother.The granddaughterFeels the same way.Because her grandmother is a control freak always telling herdaughter To run her life but her life is fucked up.The mother can't keep a job and cant payher Part of the bills because she stays in the casino all the time.The family always has to Help pay the bills sometime and the daughter's boyfriend even though he has disown place. She told the boyfriend to don't help out so he didn't and an eviction note misplace On the door and then the family helped pay the bills.This shit goes on every thermostat The mother always had her husbands to take care of the bills.The mother is a mess Always not getting along with anyone.

The day the boyfriend at the time met the lady she almost run him off.The daughter doesn't want to live with the mother but I think she is trying to make sure Her mother has a roof over her head. The family lives out of town and they told the grandmother to get her own place and give her daughter some space.The day the mother will get her own place the family dog will have his license.The mother will never get her own place because she knows she can't make it honer own. I am telling you that you cannot make this shit up.In my Kevin mussels voice.The grandmother and uncle are supposed to move down next year they removing in With the mother so the daughter can move in with the now husband. The daughter and the husband shouldn't have put themselves in that position but Her mother is fucked up.I guess love will make you do dumb shit.The mother ls being selfish because all she is doing is worrying about herself but God will Take care of that problem.I remember before they got married the daughter took boyfriend To her town and he stayed at the family home with the family the mother and the daughter Went to the casino around seven that night and didn't come back until seven that morning. The daughter doesn't play like that maybe she plays around 50 dollars. The mother gives her money to keep her to gamble far she can stay.I think the mother doesn't Care about her daughter's marriage because her marriages never worked I wonder why. I think the daughter feels sorry for her mother so she doesn't stand up when hermother I know daughters feel sorry for their mothers but live your life;your mother did,she just Made bad decisions.

 The problem in the black community is women raising a family with no man;they Don't have a man's presence because sometimes females are hard to deal with In the black community.One reason:no man in the household.Black women who Don't have an education make bad choices. I think if you served in the military,been to college,and traveled around theworld, Your selection of men would be better made because you will have a chance toMeet and communicate better when it comes to dating.I think white womenwho've been to college And the military seem to select a better spouse.Black women who ve lived in thehood their whole Life all they know is the drug boys because their education is not on a good level.I know black women who live in the hood;they work and they have a good job And they guys from their kids.I know women who don't date because they want to focus on their kids. White women-not all,but most-have a better education,and their spouse selection is better Than black women's.

The world is changing to the point where women are giving up pan men;black and white women turned towards dating women. Women know how to treat a woman,I think that isn't the truth because womenare sil getting their Asses beat and getting murdered just like if they were dating a man.I don't thinkthat is the Solution.I think if you like to date women,that is your choice,but don't think you will get treated better. I think date who you want to date,just be happy,enjoy life,and if you have kidstake care of your kids Because that is most important.I remember back in the day I was in the club and anice-looking Lady was giving me her number,and a little dude-a female-stepped up soon as I was getting the number 1 stopped,looked,and it was a female;l laughed and walked away.That girl might have gotten her ass beaten that night. if a waman is going to date a woman,make sure that is what you want to do;don't try to date both. I think if females get themselves together and only date guys with jobs and stop bringing these street guys Around their kids,I think that will make the street boys get themselves together.I know that will never happen because those in the hood who don't have a shit want that fast money.

One day the government will cut back all those food stamps and housing,and this world will turn Upside down.The jungle will begin killing and raping and robbing;it will be a mess,and it all started because these mothers didn't raise their daughters the correct way.I think the Mexicans And Asians are family people.The whites come third;their family is trash;they need to get Their shit together before it is too late.The reason I say this is the black amen,it seems like,is the Strength of the family in the hood.The black women need to step back and keeper family together. And stop fucking with these low-class niggers who are going to bring you down.I would like to see all black women step their game up. The white women have problems also,but I think they have a better selection enchantment the black women. I know there are a lot of black women who have their stuff together;l am only talking about the hood rats. You have white women who are hood rats too.The way this world is set up,awhite woman will have more opportunities than a black woman.And a white guy will gettreated better Than a black guy.The black women have to worry about Becky taking the good black men. I see nothing wrong with that;you have to shoot far the stars,and the blackwomen sleep on the good black men because they want that fast money from those drug boys.Becky sees a good opportunity and she takes advantage of a good opportunity. I remember I dated a woman who lived in the hood;she had a good gowermmentjobShe was also on section B.The lady had a son.

The only problem with her was she was high maintenance and her house wasteful. guess she was used to dating those low-class drug boys. I guess she knew that I wasn't impressed with her home so the next time l came over she Cleaned her house up and she went to the grocery store. she was close to her mother but she didn't live with her Mather.The last I heard WEE She got into a car accident,won a lot of money,and bought a house but she gained A lot of weight when I saw her pictures on Facebook. I dated another woman and she was high maintenance;I met her family and her 2daughters,15 and 16 years old. She was a stripper;she used to go out of town and leave her daughters at home.I know it is hard for black women but when you put yourself in bad situationsBecause you want that fast buck,it will ahways come out negative.The black also is included in this statement.I know when the black women andmen Make bad choices,those choices will hurt you mare than the white man or lady.Be careful and think wise.Another problem in the black community is family.Family members are hating on each other;they don't want to see one another do better. 5top the bullshit,help each other out;there is enough for us all to eat. l am going to give you a brief history an the black and white experience I have dealt with in life.I remember l used to deliver mail in the had when Worked In the post office in Las Vegas.One day l was standing by my truck and two guys Were on different sides of my truck and they decided to have a shootout;I ducked behind my truck and bullets were hitting my truck I was caught between the gunfire so I waited and then the guys took off running.I called management,and they told me to leave the area. I remember I went to deliver mail in a nice white neighborhood and a white lady came out asking me if i wanted some water;she was dressed up and had heels on. I said yes, she looked like one of those ladies in the movie.

"The Step ford Wives." I've seen this movie on TV;it was an old movie.I like watching old movies.The lady brought a glass of water out;I looked at her like "WTF?"I took the water;I thought it was going to be a bottle of water. The lady was rifting;I should have slept with her but I didn't want to put myself Ina bad situation.I never had problems meeting women.I can pick and choose so l left emerita. I remember I was in the hood again and I saw this young guy slapping his girl around. called the police and they came. The boy looked at me and he was crying;he said she started it.I told him you should Have walked away.The police came;they both were crying.
The police said sheDidn't want to press charges but he had a warrant so he went to jail.I remember another time I was delivering mail and I went to this lady's doar and she Opened the door and she said help me;he said he won't help you.I went downthe street And I called the police because if I found out he killed her I would have forgiveness myself. The police called me and told me to come around the comer and they asked me,"is this the guy?" I said yes,and they took him to jail.Call me Charleston,but what if it was your family member? The next day l saW the lady,and she said thank you.I told her to leave that guyalone; She said she will. They locked the guy up.I remember one time l was delivering mail in an American hood.

 And some girls were standing outside with some guys.One of the girts said,"The mailman is cute,"to the guys she and her friends were standing with.I went down the street to deliver the mail,and when I came back to the truck,somebody wrote "nigger"an the truck. I think it was nae of the guys who got mad at what one of the girls was saying about me. I remember one time when I was delivering mail in DC,this was before transferred My job to Vegas.I went in the hood to deliver mail,and they got mad because lid not Have a check.I had to call it in;we were told to do that,but if one of those"niggers" Would have ran up on me,I would have TMT that ass.Black people complain about How the white man treats them but then turn around and do the same to their own. I started earlier in the book talking about Denny's and Apple bee's;l just found out they Fired three workers who didn't want to serve some black customers who we rerecording it. They fired the manager and the two workers.This took place at lubber. I can't understand why black people keep eating at these restaurants;go to another Business to eat if your lazy ass doesn't want to cook;don't keep going to the someplace.Damn,you people will never get treated with respect. We need to boycott and go to black-owned businesses.I think if black people buy and cook your own food,you will save money,or if you must spend your mane,go to aback-owned Business.Black people spend a lot of money on everything;they know that,so if you boycott Their business,they will change to get your business.They don't care about you;they just Want your money because they know you will spend mare money than their white customers.

Because we like to ball;we don't know how to save money.I bet they are saying we will Get the business from these "niggers"by having Black Friday every Friday.That is what the Asians do when they make the news by slapping a black lady at the nail store,and the Guys tell the ladies to boycott.The Asians do a half-price for a day,and those dumb-ass Females will go back to the store.Ice seen it for myself.We shell over what? All these rappers spending all this money on jewelry from this Asian guy whodoesn't care about Your black ass.Take your money and invest it in land;then go over to South Africa and buy Those diamonds far cheap and get someone to make it for you far dirt cheap too.Much like right. That is why they call us "niggers";a "nigger"isn't a black person;that is what theslave owners called us.A "nigger"is a stupid-ass low-life fool;that is what you are if you keepetting these Devils pimp you.Charleston White,I see why people don't like him;he tells the truth. Cl Good fellow,he is right.He tells the truth.Less and Ring Walk Danny with Gathering Vance And Blue Blood and the Queens of Boxing,and Willie D.I like all of these people with their podcast Channels because they speak the truth. I am not putting down the black girts,but you have some fucked up white girls who do the same shit as black girls. I will break it down a little more dearly.The black mothers of today are different than The mothers from back in the day.The mothers of today are young,and they are getting younger. I know mothers who hang in the club with their daughters,smoke,and drink with their daughters.

I know a situation where a mother lets her 14-year-old daughter have a boyfriend,and he comes over to the house, And lets him come in the room and keeps the door open like that will make adherence;that Black people's shit.The girl goes over to her boyfriend's house,but because thefamily lives in a 5mall 3-bedroom apartment,the mother says nothing is going an over there because there are 7 People who live in the house.The mother treats the daughter like she is her sister;they call This sister-daughter,according to Kevin Samuel. I know there are a lot of black women who give their daughters special treatmentbecause the females don't have daddies,and little girls love their daddy.I know some mothers who let their daughters'boyfriends move in at a young age.Now you know why these young black girls have babies by the time they are 16. l am saying this doesn't happen as much in other family races because we treataur kids like they Are our friends,in my Kevin Samuel voice.This is one reason the black family has A hard time making it.Another reason there isn't any discipline in the household. The blacks let the kids run the household-all this gang-banging. The parents are to blame mast of the time;the parents grew up in that lifestyle so They pass it to their kids.The parents must let their kids grow up in a better situation. The black family,but sometimes the results can be just as bad or worse. The kids going into churches shooting black people and going into schools and mall; And grocery stores.Our kids do messed up stuff,but that right there is white people's stuff;that is what their kids do.A bill for gun violence will never happen because They are making too much money off guns;they don't care.That is the white man;he controls the guns.I think the only way you control that is you need to call the national to patrol these schools with metal detectors. The malls and churches and everywhere in a public place need metal detectors and armed security.

I also think you need to tighten up the laws;if you do anything like that,you needto be Given the death penalty.Forget staying an death row for years.I think peopleshould be Put to death right away,crazy or not;when you do something like that,it will be swift. I think this is a game;it is all about the money;the court system is bullshit.f no one goes to jail,how will they make theirmane?They need crime for wreathes The policemen,the judges,the prison system.How will they make money with no Crime? That is why they call us "niggers";a "jigger's a black person;that is what the slave owners Called us.A "nigger"is a stupid-ass low-life fool;that is what you are if you timekeeping these Devils pimp you.Charleston White,I see why people don't like him;he tells the truth. Cl Goodfellow,he is right.He tells the truth.Ness and Ring Walk Danny with TheBoxing Vaice, And Blue Blood and the Queens of Baxing,and Willie D-I like all of these peoplewith their podcast Channels because they speak the truth. l am not putting down black girls,but you have some messed up white girls whoso the same as black girls. I will break it down a little mare clearly.The black mothers of today are differentthan The mothers from back in the day.The mothers of today are young,and they are getting younger. I know mothers who hang in the club with their daughters,smoke,and drink with their daughters.

l also think you need to tighten up the laws;if you do anything like that,you needto be Given the death penalty.Forget staying an death row for years.I think peopleshould be put to death right away,crazy or not;when you do something like that,it will be swift. I think this is a game;it is all about the mane;the court system is bullshit.if no one goes to jail,how will they make their money?They need crime for the lawyers The policemen,the judges,the prison system.How will they make money with court cases AR crime?Think about it.When these kids,black or white,go to jail,their mothers are crying,"Not my baby;he wouldn't do that if you would have kept the little Motherfucker home and not in the streets at 15;he'd still be living or not in jail." it started earlier,the black or white family with no daddy at home. That is the biggest problem in the black family-not enough James Evans in the household. want to talk about the black mothers who live with their grown daughters.How do you think your daughter wile be able to meet a man and have a nice life if you are living with your mother?I think that isn't fair because the mother had perchance to have a relationship; it didn't work,so give your daughter a chance to make her relationship work.The white mothers want their daughters to meet a husband and have kids and buy house. The black mother wants to stay in her daughter's life and raise her grand kids-motall mothers Are like that.The ones that are want to be controlling.I know a case where the mother always Was trying to chase the man away.The mother made mistakes in her life,so why are you Trying to run your daughter's life?I've been seeing this in a lot of black families. I think from a man's view,if you meet a girl and she lives with her mother before take it to the next level, make sure you and that women get your own place before you marry her.

l am saying this isn't always the reasan why mothers live with their daughters.Themain reason is this:women are single,trying to raise the kids by herself,and hermother has to come in And help her raise the kids.Women need to do a hetter joh meeting men;everyman that looks nice And has a nice car ar a good job is not always the perfect match.Men Who have allaf these Things going on in his life means he has a lot of women,ar he doesn't want tobe Married, Or he is a control freak.I think women should slow down and try to find out why this man Is single. I think if you take your time,you will find the reason he might sit on the toilet when he pees. Amen who like to date women can find the same abuse in dating a woman just like dating a man. 1 knew a gird who told me her girlfriend is very abusive,and she had to get out ofthe relationship Because she got tired of getting her ass beat. Men who date men go through the same treatment;men can be very abusive also;hear a lot of stories.Women also need to bring the right man around their daughters. I want to get back on the subject of races;I think I touch a lot of subjects,but let'sget a little deeper.I want to go back and talk about the movie business.I wasreading that Elvis had a manager That took him through bad contracts.I don't know if it was bad like theblack entertainers. Prince had a problem with his masters,M had a problem with his masters,as well as Whitney Houston. lames Brown and a lot of entertainers,and it has been said most of these entertainers lost their lives over this subject.

I heard the doctor who was locked up behind MI's death has left the country and has never Been heard of again when he was freed from jail.They say he was given a large sum AF Manet for pulling that off.I hope that isn't true because he will be haunted for thereat of his life. Money doesn't have a color when it comes to black or white;they will take youout fgi The green buck.The devil is alive,and we know who he is. The new police bill-this bill should have come out a long time ago.The bill cameout During election time;I wonder why. Can't see how law enforcement personnel can be fired in one state and then hired in another. You can't do that in the post office. I think they need to put all law enforcement in a database,and if your name comes up,you need To be fired.I think they should pay police a bonus if you report your partner committing a crime. What's called snitching on the street could save lives and get bad cops off the streets. I hope all the bad policemen and women would be taken care of when they go see Their maker,the Devil.And I am pretty sure they already did. The person to be in law enforcement should be someone who grew up with all races. You can't put a white cop in the hood if he's never been around black people.All they know about black people is what they see an TV or in the movies.I don't have anything against cops,just the bad Ames. Female cops are the worst;they always think they have to be tough to prove Themselves,especially the white ans who think they are men.I guess you have Black female cops who act the same way.The system will never change;everyone's about money that is why it will never change as long as they make money; it will always stay.

The same,but it is good to tall about when election rolls around.The prison system will never work;it's a money maker.The problem is we are spending too much Money and time helping other countries. Help our people out first;target those other people;they don't care about us;welcome first.I don't Understand.I think we have a lot of kids and homeless people living on the street.This country is too weak.I want to go back and touch on kids;most people raise their kid: The way they take care of themselves.All kids believe in Santa Claus,so let your kids believe in Santa Claus. When your kid reaches that age that you did and stops believing,they will do the same. I know white people who didn't like anyone who isn't white,and they raised their kids that way. kids will grow up and turn into adults;they will make their own minds up.Thenone day they will date whoever they want to.If Becky starts dating a black guy,that's when the Problems start with the white family if they have a baby.I am pretty sure some families cut their Kids out of the will. I think I covered a lot of topics about racism,but I could sit here all day and cover this topic. I would like to state one more time:The black race spends a lot of money unclothes,food, And cars.Men and women,it makes no sense;then we would go to all these fancy Restaurants,and we get treated like crap.Denny's,Apple bee's,I could go on and an. I think it's the people who work there who are racists;they need to fire those people when They get a complaint.So why are we supporting those places,black people?some of you Guys are saying it never happened to me.I think if we band together and ate our own places, and if you have the money, hire the cook.

The people don't care;they are stupid as fuck-that's where the problem commemorate. The rappers are killing each other left and right over dumb shit. I don't understand;there is enough maney to go around for everybody.I don'thave to do any name-dropping;you know who l am talking about-your favorite rapper, Teaching these kids,girls to boys,all this bullshit.The kids know the songs theoretician schoolwork. The young maters are to blame,and their mothers are to blame,and most of these kids Who are failures,you can blame that on the parents,black to white.The day will come when this world will change;it is changing right as I speak,andall of these Dumb kids and parents will get caught crying for help;it will be too late,and cannot wait. When they have problems,you can blame that on the parents because most kidsare not smart enough to catch on to life.Smaller kids are more respectful than the older Kids;that is the way this ward is;that is why you have to teach these kids when they are young because when they get to be 13,it is over. I'd also like to talk about what I heard Trump was talking about.I heard someone ask him if we were going To have another war.Trump said the war that we will have will be one of the worst wars of all time. I understand you can't go around thinking of the end of the world,but think of all the young people who Are not educated,black to white,who will survive.All the young kids,some educated,then others. Then the kids that are not educated,black,white,and all races.This is why weaned to educate ou Kids and stop thinking about black and white.

The death toll will rise,black,white,blue,and green;it won't matter to strapless because if you have money,you think you willies forever and you are better than most.The people who don't have money don't care;they are trying to survive,living day to day. The next iew years will be the hardest in life for people who don't have money.God bless and all praise to Allah.I will add one more problem I know I mentionedearlier about Black women so in love with these designer bags,I don't see anything wrong with that,but When you get kicked off the plane,go to jail over a designer bag,I think somethings going On in that lady's head.I read about these problems with our black women everyday. The lady was black;she was a veteran;if she was active,they would have kicked her out of The service.I will say our young people need to get it together cal quick.
I bet most young people don't have a clue what is going an today.Trump said NikkiHaley Wants to raise the retirement age to 77 years ald because we are living to that age. okay,let's say she won;people will be working their whole lives until they die.That is why these kids Need to pay attention to what is going on because this will hurt you guys in the long run. The people of today need to wake up because most of us are uneducated and they're not Paying attention and if that happens,crime will shoot through the roof.God bless And all praise to Allah.

THE
END

BY: DeHaven J Alexander